D1741691

First published in 2001 by Brimax
an imprint of Octopus Publishing Group Ltd
2-4 Heron Quays, London E14 4JP
© Octopus Publishing Group Ltd
Printed in China

My First Prayers

All Things Bright and Beautiful

Includes:

- All Things Bright and Beautiful
- All Creatures Great and Small
- All Things Wise and Wonderful
- The Lord God Made Us All

Illustrated by Stephanie Longfoot

All things bright and beautiful,
We see God's wonder every day,

He fills our world with brilliance,
And does it all His way.

In winter He creates the frost,
Covering all in sparkling white,

In spring He makes the flowers grow,
Blessing us with His gift of life.

In summer time He ripens fruit,
Giving food for everyone,

Then the leaves tumble and fall,
And we have lots of fun.

He puts the green grass in the fields,
The animals that run and play,

He fills each child with laughter,
And puts beauty in our days.

God paints the rainbow in the sky,
The stars that shine so bright,

He fills our days with sunshine,
And the moon that lights the night.

All creatures great and small,
Wherever they may live,

Below, above or with us,
To them His love God gives.

In the sky He put birds,
They love to soar and fly,

They fill our world with song,
As they go gliding by.

In the sea He put fish,
They like to swim all day,

They sparkle in the sunlight,
And play beneath the waves.

On the land He put mankind,
Animals and insects together,

Who run and jump, and walk and hop,
In every kind of weather.

God filled His world with creatures,
Ponies large and kittens small,

We are each part of His family,
Birds, fish, animals, all.

All things wise and wonderful
Surround us every day,

They help to fill our lives with joy,
Thank you, dear God, we say.

You give us friends who care for us,
A family to love,

They hold our hands, they understand,
Like you our Lord above.

Dear God you gave us Mother,
She helps to make things right,

We love to make her happy,
And she loves to hold us tight.

Dear God you gave us Father,
He knows what's good and bad,

We try to make him proud of us,
He cheers us when we're sad.

Dear God you give us people,
So wise and wonderful,

Doctors, teachers, parents, friends,
And you to love us all.

The Lord God made us all,
Every shape and every size,

He put His creatures on the land,
Into the sea and sky.

He made the mountains high and wide,
He made the raindrops small,

He made each flower different,
The Lord God made them all.

He made every person special,
He gave us each a different face,

He made us all in different shades,
The Lord God made each race.

He made each person think and feel,
Taught us how to love and share,

He helped each one of us believe,
For us the Lord God cares.

He is beside us every day,
He is in all we see and do.

He made each animal, tree and bird,
The Lord God made you too.